D0175061

LINES FOR ALL OCCASIONS

Excuses & Lies

KNOCK
KNOCK®
VENICE, CALIFORNIA

Created and published by Knock Knock
Distributed by Who's There, Inc.
Venice, CA 90291
knockknockstuff.com

This book is a work of humor meant solely for
entertainment purposes. Actually utilizing the
lines contained herein may be illegal or lead to
bodily injury. The publisher and anyone associated
with the production of this book do not advocate
breaking the law. In no event will Knock Knock be
liable to any reader for any damages, including
direct, indirect, incidental, special, consequential,
or punitive arising out of or in connection with the
use of the lines contained in this book. So there.

ISBN: 978-160106057-0
UPC: 825703-50107-0

Contents

"She probably lost your number."

Introduction

Excuses and lies are a necessary
part of life. Six-month-olds begin
their careers as proud fibbers with
fake laughter and cries, and it's all
downhill from there. In fact, if
anyone says they don't lie, they're
lying. Scientists have demonstrated
that excuses and lies paved our
evolutionary path by allowing us
simultaneously to advance our own
interests and to cement our role
within our group. Would we ever

get our dream job if we said we couldn't type? Could we maintain our clique status if we said "I hate your new haircut?" Successful lying promotes survival of the fittest—the fittest, of course, are the liars.

Forget about guilt—we're born liars and we die liars. What matters is how we lie in between. The overwhelming daily demands of our personal and professional lives are simply too much to handle without excuses and lies. When it comes to saving friendships, dignity, or our own skins, honesty is, quite simply, overrated. Being truthful can ruin marriages, sabotage negotiations, and possibly bring an end to the world as we know it. In his essay "On the Decay of the Art of Lying," no lesser light than Mark Twain acknowledged, "Everybody lies—every day; every hour; awake; asleep; in his dreams; in his joy; in his mourning." The question is not whether to lie or tell the truth— the question is how to lie well.

While all of us are liars, not everybody experiences the easy flow of words to lips, and that's where the Lines for All Occasions series comes in, arming you with verbatim sentences to recite in diverse situations. These handy, pocket-sized books can be carried with confidence as a reference for solutions to modern-life dilemmas. In *Excuses and Lies for All Occasions*, you'll find help for the workplace, friendships and dating, family and other loved ones, your own inner thoughts, and infractions such as unpaid bills. Finally, because famous people lie more than the average prevaricator, we present you with an inspiring panoply of excuses and lies from the best of the best.

Delivering a deception is crucial to its reception. The worse the falsehood, the more sincere you must appear. Though the words contained in this book will help you with lying panache, the execution is still up to you. To amplify the many tips sprinkled among these pages, following are a few basic principles to keep in mind. Add details to your lie; the more realism you lend, the more believable your story. Make sure your lies reflect your personality; some of the lines in this book might not be quite "you," but it's possible to rephrase slightly to add your own flair. Don't stumble over your words; be prepared beforehand so that you can fluently narrate your fallacious tale. Add half-truths or even whole truths into your lies so that the two become indistinguishable and one adds veracity to the other; before long, you won't even know the difference. Finally, keep track of your lies. Liars are most frequently caught because they tell two different stories at two different times, so memory is crucial.

From the most stuttering rationalizer to the baldest-faced fabricator, *Excuses and Lies* will not only provide the best falsehoods for the widest variety of situations, it will help those who still value honesty to shed that useless mantle and get with the human program. Whether or not you believe all this, of course, is up to you—for all you know, we could be lying.

THE WORKPLACE

When you just can't manage it

FOR SOME REASON, WHEN YOU GET a job, the expectation is that you will arrive on time and show up every day; overall, most managers assume that work will be your priority. That's understandable, because you probably lied to get hired in the first place. Studies show that most resumés are full of misrepresentations: 71 percent increase tenures of previous jobs,

Don't Work, Just Lie

Studies show that one-quarter to one-third of all workers tell lies to explain their tardiness or absence. When dallying away from the office, solid excuses and lies are critical, as the same data showed that most managers would be likely to fire employees who were repeatedly late or absent without explanation. Fortunately, nearly three-quarters of employers polled indicated they generally believe the excuses their employees give.

64 percent exaggerate accomplishments, 60 percent overstate the size of departments managed, 52 percent cite partial degrees as full, and 48 percent inflate salary history.

No matter your stellar background, sometimes work will be incompatible with your personal needs, and that's where workplace excuses and lies come in. The day-to-day grind

practically requires that you fudge
the truth. Whether it's explaining
your tardiness, coming up with an
excuse for playing hooky, buying
extra time for a deadline, blaming
technology, or providing context
for why you've fallen asleep on
the job, this chapter will equip
you with every line necessary.

Meeting your own needs serves a
larger purpose. You can't perform
with all the pressure of punctuality
and due dates, five-day workweeks
and missed sleep. Often, it's just
plain prudent to take a three-day
weekend. And a spontaneous after-
noon off will probably refresh you
so much that your productivity will
skyrocket. When you get down to
it, your tardiness and absenteeism
are for the good of the team—but
they don't have to know that.

Tardiness

I'm okay now, but I actually
threw up on the way over here.

I couldn't find my keys anywhere.

You should have *seen* the line at
Starbucks, and you do not want
me here without caffeine.

My cat got out and I chased her
all over the neighborhood.

I got pulled over. The idiot cop took
forever. Fortunately, I didn't get a ticket.

I wanted to wait until the
laxative kicked in.

The toilet overflowed and I had
to wait for the plumber.

A dive-bombing bird kept
me captive, a prisoner in
my own home!

———•◦•———

I had another panic attack.
Don't worry—it wasn't about work.

———•◦•———

Some moron stopped short
and I slammed on the brakes,
spilling my coffee all over myself.
Not only do I have third-degree
burns in unmentionable places,
I had to go home and change.

———•◦•———

I checked a friend into rehab
on my way to the office.

———•◦•———

For some reason, my alarm
didn't go off this morning!

———•◦•———

It took an hour to get over
my fear of success.

Some Jehovah's Witnesses came to the
door and I could *not* get rid of them.

———•◦•———

I was dealing with a personal matter.

———•◦•———

It takes hours to look this good!

Hooky

The cable's out, and I have to wait
all day for the technician to arrive.

———•◦•———

It's most contagious in the
early stages, and I don't want to
expose everyone at the office.

———•◦•———

My husband's eighty-four-year-old
great-aunt died—suddenly!

———•◦•———

I can't find my car.

———•◦•———

I feel a migraine coming on.

My kid is sick.

————•—•————

My babysitter is sick.

————•—•————

Someone else's kid is sick, and just because I'm single and childless doesn't mean I can't stay home.

————•—•————

Two words—bad clams.

Tip: Track Your Absences

While it may be tempting to utilize the complete arsenal of excuses presented here, do exercise some caution when skipping work. Keep track of your "sick" days so that you don't overdo it. Days flanking holidays are scrutinized, so don't take too many of those. Be careful about absences that dovetail with publicly known interests of yours—for example, if you are known to be an avid skier, don't call in sick after a huge snowstorm.

My boyfriend is having his first
root canal and I need to nurse
him through the pain.

———•◦•———

My vet said I had to watch
her all day to make sure she
doesn't have a bad reaction
to the medication.

———•◦•———

My briefcase was filled with
work I took home, and when
I bent down to pick it up,
I threw my back out.

———•◦•———

I need a day just for me.

———•◦•———

I'm too fat to fit into
my work clothes.

———•◦•———

My crotch itches.

———•◦•———

I just can't stop crying.

Missed Deadline

Didn't we cancel that project?

———•◦•———

I need an assistant to help me
keep track of things like this.

———•◦•———

Nothing short of perfect
will do for you.

———•◦•———

I left it at my friend's house and
she's out of town for a month.

———•◦•———

I have it in my calendar for *next* week.

———•◦•———

Everybody else failed to get
me what I needed in time.

———•◦•———

I tried so hard, but no matter
what I did, I couldn't finish the
project *and* take my government-
mandated ten-minute breaks.

Truth Fascism

Alexander Kuzmin, mayor of the Siberian town of Megion, has banned city workers from using certain excuses, including "I don't know," "It's not my job," "It's impossible," and "I'm having lunch." A framed list of all twenty-seven prohibited excuses hangs next to Kuzmin's office. Those who refuse to uphold the ban "will near the moment of their departure." Fortunately, in America excuse-making is an inalienable right—especially for bureaucrats.

You didn't authorize overtime.

———•—•———

Every time I thought about the project, it stressed me out.

———•—•———

Do you want it fast, or do you want it right?

———•—•———

The schedule was completely unrealistic.

It's a moving target, and I want
the information to be as up-
to-the-minute as possible.

I delegated that!

I have it right here. Wait—
where did that file go?

I'm waiting for the muse to strike.

I've determined that work
just isn't necessary.

I did my best. That's all you can ask.

20th-Century Scapegoat: Technology

I accidentally deleted it.

I ran out of paper.

Someone hacked into the file server
over SSH using a crypt-hash attack
and placed a root kit that caused
a buffer overrun precipitating a
failure of AFP. As a result, the server
unmounted, and unfortunately
I hadn't saved my document.

———•◦•———

Didn't you get it? I emailed the
whole thing to you from my
home computer last night.

———•◦•———

Really? It works on my machine.

———•◦•———

I totally, like, fried my motherboard.

———•◦•———

The file was mysteriously corrupted.

———•◦•———

I do *not* view porn at work!

———•◦•———

I have bad news—the
system error was fatal.

Carpal tunnel—it's spreading
through the entire office.

Your email must have gone
into my spam folder.

I'll have my IT guy look into
it and get back to you.

I'm afraid it's Sad Mac.

One word—Microsoft.

Sleeping on the Job

My keyboard was making
the strangest noise.

So funny that you would walk in at
this very moment! I was just meditating
on the strategic initiatives with
respect to our core competencies.

I find that a fifteen-minute power nap improves my overall time management immeasurably.

———•———

One second I was smelling my pen, and the next second you were waking me up!

———•———

My chiropractor told me to rest my neck periodically in order to avoid having to make a worker's comp claim.

———•———

Some idiot made decaf.

———•———

Could you turn the heat down a tad?

———•———

I keep taking swills from the flask in my desk drawer. For some reason, it makes me sleepy.

———•———

I ate too many carbs at lunch.

It's okay. I'm still clocking
them as billable hours.

———◦◦◦———

By accident I took the
nighttime medicine.

———◦◦◦———

It's my break, and I can do
what I want with it!

———◦◦◦———

Amen.

Out-Teching Your Boss

The office offers countless technical resources
that make it appear that you're hard at work—
a necessity for the two hours a day the average employee spends on personal activities.
Options include "boss" or "panic" buttons
that, when clicked, immediately cover any
recreational screens with fake spreadsheets;
digital recordings of office noises to make
you sound busy; or the telephone for pretend
conversations, a tried but true standby.

LIKED ONES

When the truth will hurt

IN THE COURSE OF NORMAL SOCIAL
interaction, honesty is overrated.
Indeed, if the truth were consis-
tently told, the result would be
social anarchy—the end of friendships, correspondence, entertaining,
cohabitation, and dating. Social lies
are frequently euphemized as tact
or diplomacy (another lie—because
what are those but misrepresentations or lies of omission?). However

Everybody's Doing It

University of Massachusetts psychologist
Robert Feldman studied undergraduates
to determine everyday lying frequency. He
discovered that 60 percent of the subjects
lied during a ten-minute conversation; indeed,
they told an average of two to three lies per
encounter. He also learned that motivations
for lying split along gender lines: women
tended to lie to make others feel good, while
men lied to make themselves look better.

you justify your necessary prevarication, this chapter will provide you
with the verbal ammunition for just
about any communal situation.

Perhaps most closely related to
tact and diplomacy is the category
known as white lies, those uttered
to make someone feel good (or not
bad)—refraining from calling a
new haircut a chop job, for example.

Gray lies dig a bit more into relationship dynamics you'd rather not broach, such as assuring a gossipy friend of your trust in her. Amidst our busy, transcontinental, multimedia lives, staying in touch has become a particular onus, for which an arsenal of excuses is essential. The modern lifestyle also requires that we limit the number of invitations we accept—and extend. Finally, dating and dating sex introduce a host of opportunities for excuses and lies—and undoubtedly this misrepresentation is reciprocal.

The first lie we tell in our social lives is "Fine"; the answer to "How are you?" Why stop there? Excuses and lies grease the skids of social interaction, and if your social life isn't greasy, you've got some work to do—and these are the lines to help.

Friendship: White Lies

You made that all by yourself?
It looks so professional!

———•————

No one would even notice.

———•————

I love it!

———•————

Your taste is so eclectic!

———•————

The decor really reflects your personality.

———•————

There's only one word for
this—interesting.

———•————

I think it's the best thing
you've ever written.

———•————

Remember—
looks aren't everything.

They look totally real!

It's probably just water weight.

That is *so* funny.

That is *so* smart.

You don't look a day
over twenty-nine.

Everyone's a little crazy.

Friendship: Gray Lies

Thanks for being so honest.

I'm sure he's just really busy.

I didn't know it was a secret!

I won't tell if you won't.

———•◦•———

I did it for your own good.

———•◦•———

I really like your husband.

———•◦•———

I really like your wife.

———•◦•———

Of course I'm not jealous.

———•◦•———

I'd tell you if I thought
you needed therapy.

———•◦•———

You'll make a great parent.

———•◦•———

I can always count on you.

———•◦•———

It was just a misunderstanding.

———•◦•———

I didn't mean it.

BFF!

———•◦•———

Nothing's wrong.

Out of Touch

I never got your message.

———•◦•———

I've been *so* crazy at work and just haven't had a single moment to call you.

Lying Makes the Man

According to David Livingstone Smith, author of *Why We Lie*, all lies perform one of two necessary functions: they either enable us to fit into society or they advance self-preservation. Psychologist Robert Feldman discovered that teens who lie most convincingly tend to be the most popular. As Feldman states, lying is "a social skill." Probably because of their aptitude for non-verbal cues, Feldman also found that girls lie better than boys.

As soon as I hit my deadlines,
we'll have dinner.

———•◦•———

It's so great to hear your
voice! However, I'm in the
middle of something.

———•◦•———

We're in the honeymoon stage;
it won't always be this way.

———•◦•———

The wedding planning is
taking over my life.

———•◦•———

The children have taken over my life.

———•◦•———

I can't find a babysitter.

———•◦•———

I've developed an addiction to crack;
unfortunately, it's very time-consuming.

———•◦•———

It's a very busy time of year for me.

Has it really been that long?
It doesn't feel like it.

———◆———

There's just so much TV to watch,
I don't seem to get out much.

———◆———

My PDA was stolen,
so I had to make new friends.

———◆———

Let's meet up after the holidays.

Turning Down Invitations

I'm going to be sick that night.

———◆———

I'd love to, but I have to work.

———◆———

I'm completely and
utterly exhausted.

———◆———

I don't have TiVo.

Tip: Texting Off the Phone

Just because you answered the phone doesn't mean you're available. With long-winded friends, never feel like you have to talk beyond your comfort zone. Simply hang up then send a text message such as "Phone crappy—TTYL" ("talk to you later"). For more impact, shout, "Oh my God! I have to go!" then hang up. A few minutes later, text "Sorry. Everything's okay. TTYL." After that, a good old-fashioned game of phone-tag can keep you safe for weeks.

I have to wake up early the next day.

That's my weekly
night for alone time.

I don't believe in Evites.

My significant other is
having a total meltdown
and needs my help.

I fell down and hurt myself.

———◦•◦———

I can't be around people
who are drinking.

———◦•◦———

I can't be around people
who are eating.

———◦•◦———

I don't have anything to wear.

———◦•◦———

The environment is being
destroyed, and you expect
me to celebrate?

Unvitations

It's just an intimate gathering.

———◦•◦———

It's only family.

———◦•◦———

It's only immediate family.

It's a whole different crowd.

———•◦•———

I'm not inviting anyone from work.

———•◦•———

It's in honor of someone
you don't know.

———•◦•———

I don't have enough chairs.

———•◦•———

It's more of a religious
ritual than a party.

———•◦•———

It's more of a meeting
than a party.

———•◦•———

Your invitation must have
gotten lost in the mail.

———•◦•———

I invited your ex instead.

———•◦•———

Party? What party?

Roommates

I cleaned the toilet last time.

———•———

Those aren't my dirty dishes.

———•———

I have no idea how
your shoes got ruined.

———•———

I didn't think you would mind.

———•———

I totally paid that bill.

———•———

I'll pay you back next week.

———•———

That beer was yours?

———•———

I thought you weren't coming
home until tomorrow.

———•———

I'm just having a few people over.

I don't know
whose vomit that is.

———•———

He hasn't "moved in with us."
He just sleeps over every night.

———•———

We weren't having sex
in the shower—we were
trying to conserve water.

Getting Out of Dates

I'm gay.

———•———

I'm straight.

———•———

I'm married.

———•———

I don't date.

———•———

You're not my type.

My therapist says
you're not my type.

———◆———

I'm just not ready yet.

———◆———

I'm so attracted to
you that it scares me.

———◆———

I don't eat in front of people.

Rescue Call

Technology can save you from a bad date or
a boring dinner party. Various online services
will call your phone at a pre-arranged time
with a rescue call. You don't even have to
think of what to say—the recorded voice will
prompt you to repeat scripted lines, resulting
in a realistic impression that your roommate
is locked out, a relative has been taken ill, or
there's a babysitter emergency. If you happen
to be having a good time, just hang up.

You can't afford me.

———•———

You're too good for me.

———•———

I have to wash my hair.

———•———

I know I'm just a barista,
but I'm focusing on my
career right now.

Date Sex

Okay, just a quick drink.

———•———

The divorce is in the works.

———•———

I've never done anything
like this before.

———•———

We don't have to do anything
more than cuddling.

I really think this
could go somewhere.

———•———

You are *so* hot.

———•———

Of course I'll respect
you in the morning.

———•———

The clinic says I'm clear.

———•———

It's only a cold sore.

———•———

I'm allergic to latex.

———•———

You should go pro.

———•———

This has never
happened to me before.

———•———

I'll call you.

LOVED ONES

When you care enough to prevaricate

THOSE WHOM WE HOLD NEAR AND
dear will, from time to time, create
the need for clever lies and excuses.
This doesn't mean you love them
any less—on the contrary, you
dissemble precisely because you
love them so much, whether to
protect their feelings, preserve
idealism, or guard against painful
truths. If you didn't lie, most likely
they'd eventually cease to love *you*.

Tip: Body Language

When delivering a lie—especially to the loved ones who know you best—avoid non-verbal "tells." Lying cues include forced smiles (real smiles involve the muscles around the eyes), formal phrasing (eschewing contractions such as "don't" and "can't"), pitch changes (non-lying vocal levels are relatively even), and erratic eye contact (truth tellers maintain contact, occasionally looking up and to the left, while liars look down and to the right).

Parents lie to their children for so many reasons. Perhaps a child isn't yet ready for induction into the mores of adulthood. Maybe a child deserves to have a myth remain intact. Finally, there isn't a parent alive who hasn't lied simply for expediency. Fortunately, these lies have a positive impact on children, as it aids them in becoming better liars, stimulating their imaginations and preparing them for the world. Of course, children turn right around and lie to their parents, and this chapter includes some sterling nuggets of filial deception.

It's between couples, however, that the richest opportunities for fabrication arise, whether around everyday interactions, sex, or actual infidelity. If partners told one another everything in the daily struggle to stay together, the divorce rate would be higher than 0.38 percent per capita per year, and that's not even including serious relationships that haven't been ratified by official marriage.

The moral of this story? If you love someone, lie—and if you really love them, lie with scripted wit and creativity.

Parents to Children

We're almost there.

There are no onions
in the lasagna.

It tastes just like chicken.

Santa Claus is coming!

The Tooth Fairy just knows.

He went to doggy heaven.

This hurts me more
than it hurts you.

Daddy was just giving mommy
a special backrub.

Yes, he's your real father.

It's what's on the
inside that counts.

The best things in life are free.

You can do anything you
want if you really try.

You can talk to me
about anything.

It's perfectly normal.

If you don't go to college, you'll
end up pumping gas for a living.

You can't do anything with
a liberal-arts degree.

If you have sex before you're
married, you'll go to hell.

Smoking marijuana is one step
away from heroin addiction.

Of course I trust you.

Children to Parents

I didn't do it.

Someone made me do it.

My friend's mom let *him* do it.

Everybody's doing it.

No one else's parents ever do that.

Dad said I could do it.

Mom said I could do it.

———•—•———

You didn't tell me not to do it.

———•—•———

I only did it once.

———•—•———

I learned it from you.

———•—•———

She started it.

Born Liars

Humans begin lying shortly after birth. Six-month-old babies get into the game through fake crying and laughing. Two months later, they've added concealment and distraction. At two years old, toddlers bluff, and by their fourth birthdays they've discovered the advantages of flattery. Before they're ten, children will have learned to cover up a lie—well in advance of their teenage years, when all that prevarication will truly come in handy.

It was already broken.

———•———

I didn't hear you.

———•———

I don't feel well.

———•———

We're studying.

———•———

We're not doing anything.

———•———

Of course grownups will be there.

———•———

I don't know.

———•———

Nothing.

———•———

Nowhere.

———•———

You can trust me.

Couples: Everyday

This isn't new—I've had it forever.

———•—•———

Your mother is
welcome anytime.

———•—•———

That dinner was delicious.

———•—•———

No, that doesn't
make you look fat.

———•—•———

I like you with a few curves.

———•—•———

No, that really doesn't
make you look fat.

———•—•———

I don't mind if you go out
with your friends.

———•—•———

I like your friends.

Lying Hall of Fame

Baron Munchausen, an eighteenth-century German raconteur, told such tall tales that they merited compilation in *The Adventures of Baron Munchausen*. His name was later immortalized in Munchausen syndrome, a psychopathology in which someone induces or fakes illness to gain sympathy and attention. And when caregivers, especially parents, inflict or project ailments onto those under their care, they're diagnosed with Munchausen syndrome by proxy.

I'll be ready in a minute.

I'll do it in a minute.

I've never heard that story before!

Everybody thought it was hilarious.

I really want to know.

Of course I'm listening.

Nothing's wrong.

Yes, dear.

Couples: Sex

I had a hard day at work.

I'm tired.

I'm sleeping.

I have a headache.

Maybe later.

I was in the mood—
yesterday.

I ate too much for dinner.

———•◆•———

Try me again in the morning.

———•◆•———

My head says yes but my
yeast infection says no.

———•◆•———

You look so hot in
those flannel pajamas.

———•◆•———

I need you to pump me up for
my presentation tomorrow.

———•◆•———

It'll only take a minute.

———•◆•———

Nobody can hear us.

———•◆•———

I just want to express
my love for you.

———•◆•———

I bought you flowers.

I'll take care of everything—
you can just lie there.

If we don't do it soon,
we'll forget how.

Couples: Cheating

I have to work late.

The Internet provides a different
kind of outlet for me.

I'll get in bed in a second—
I just need to shower first.

Can you believe my boss scheduled
another business trip?

Oh, we were just joking
around in those emails.

We're just friends.

I'm not in the least
bit attracted to him.

I'm not in the least
bit attracted to her.

I'm not in the least
bit attracted to them.

The lipstick on my collar? My mother's!

It just happened.

I was seduced!

I've never been that drunk before.

I'm a child of divorce—
what did you expect?

I wanted to buy a Porsche
instead, but we can't afford it.

———•◦•———

Everybody does it.

———•◦•———

It didn't mean anything.

———•◦•———

I'll never do it again.

Animal Instinct

Your pets may not always be telling you the
truth—lying pervades the animal kingdom.
Some frogs lower their croaks to imitate larger
frogs, thus attracting more females. Mother
birds have been known to feign broken wings to
divert predatory attention away from the nest. In
one of the most overt displays of cross-species
lying, Koko, a sign-language-speaking gorilla,
tore the sink off the wall of her pen and then,
referring to her pet kitten, signed "Cat did it."

SELF-DECEPTIONS

When it's so not your fault

DESPITE ALL THE ADVANCES MADE IN the therapeutic industry during the twentieth century, with its devout advocacy of self-awareness, inner-honesty is overrated. If you really believed that you'd never exercise, save money, find God, or recycle, you'd be so bogged down with guilt and self-loathing that it would be impossible to get out of bed in the morning. People who lie to

Tip: Fake It 'Til You Make It

Whether it's "I'll quit tomorrow" or "I deserve those shoes," spurious thoughts may help you achieve success. Books like *The Secret* recycle the concept of positive thinking, dubbing it the "law of attraction" or "intentionality"—if you think it, it will come—and there's some neurological data to back that up. Further, studies have shown that happy people are less honest with themselves than depressives, just one more reason to self-deceive.

themselves are more confident and self-assured than those who grapple with the truth of their own inadequacies. For true mental health, it's imperative to self-deceive; scientific studies actually support this.

While there are many ways to trick yourself into believing your own nonsense, the most fruitful and universally applicable is reliance on the concept of tomorrow: the metaphorical tomorrow, meaning not now. Tomorrow frees you of responsibilities and allows you to do whatever it is you *want* to do, guilt-free, whether you crave food, sleep, cigarettes, heroin, shoes, or disposable dinnerware. You can start, quit, save, repent, contribute, or follow your dreams—tomorrow. Tomorrow is, in fact, the self-liar's best friend.

If tomorrow were the only weapon in the arsenal of self-deception, however, this chapter would not be such a wealth of witty absolution, useful whether you're one of the few unhappy souls who never lie to themselves or, like most of us, you could just stand to brush up on your self-deception techniques.

Diet and Exercise

I'm way too busy to start
anything right now.

———•———

A pint is a single serving.

———•———

I'll work out extra hard tomorrow.

———•———

I'm going through a rough time.

———•———

I deserve a treat.

———•———

Studies show that dark
chocolate is good for you.

———•———

With the kids, the job,
the house, and the spouse,
who has time to exercise?

———•———

It might rain.

It's fat-free!

———•—•———

It's carb-free!

———•—•———

If I could afford a personal
chef and trainer like Oprah, I'd
be in great shape, too.

———•—•———

I feel like I'm coming
down with something.

———•—•———

It's too hot.

———•—•———

It's too cold.

———•—•———

I'm out of sunscreen.

———•—•———

I don't fit into my
exercise clothes.

———•—•———

I'll start tomorrow.

Vices

I'll quit smoking when I have kids.

I'm just a social smoker—
I never buy a pack.

If I quit smoking, I'll get fat.

But American Spirit
is all-natural!

Red wine prevents heart attacks,
but you have to drink a lot of it.

Okay, just one drink.

I need to drink—my job
is really stressful.

It's not drinking alone if
you have the TV on.

I'm just a social drinker.

————•◦•————

I don't drink before noon.

————•◦•————

It's noon somewhere.

————•◦•————

I'd rather die young and high
than old and sober.

Tomorrow…It'll Be Good

If you wait long enough, your vices may turn
into virtues, allowing you to funnel your
excuses and lies into other areas. In 2006,
coffee was touted for raising mood and reduc-
ing disease risk; one medical review claimed
"the more you drink, the better." In 2007,
headlines celebrated the health benefits of
red wine and chocolate, and now it appears
that overweight people may live longer. Could
cigarettes be far behind?

It's not like I use
needles or anything.

———•◦•———

I'm not addicted.

———•◦•———

It's not illegal.

———•◦•———

It shouldn't be illegal.

———•◦•———

You only live once.

———•◦•———

I'll stop tomorrow.

Money

I can always return it.

———•◦•———

If I didn't spend a hundred dollars,
I couldn't get the free gift!

———•◦•———

I had a coupon.

It was on sale.

———•———

I had a coupon
and it was on sale.

———•———

It's an early birthday present.

———•———

I just got my tax refund.

———•———

I deserve it.

———•———

It's one of a kind!

———•———

It will only appreciate in value.

———•———

Shopping is good for the
country—George Bush said so.

———•———

They offered me
interest-free financing.

Pledge Allegiance

Shopping is good for the economy. After the September 11th terrorist attacks, President George Bush told the country to "Get down to Disney World . . . and enjoy life, the way we want it to be enjoyed." British prime minister Tony Blair exhorted the world "to shop" to thwart recession. Mayor Rudolph Giuliani called New Yorkers "the best shoppers in the world" and urged them to action. When it comes to spending, patriotism is still the best excuse.

That's why God invented credit cards.

———•◦•———

Everybody spends beyond their means—it's the American way.

———•◦•———

The kids can't go to school dressed like paupers.

———•◦•———

My neighbor has two.

I'll stop going out to dinner
and buying lattes and I'll
bring my lunch every day.

———•◦•———

I won't buy anything new for a year.

———•◦•———

It makes me look hot.

———•◦•———

It's cheaper than surgery.

———•◦•———

It makes me feel good.

———•◦•———

It's cheaper than therapy.

Spirituality

I know God says "Love
thy neighbor," but he hasn't
met my neighbor.

———•◦•———

All's fair when it's us against them.

Because I'm morally and spiritually
superior and I'm going to heaven,
I have the right to judge others.

———•———

I have no latent homosexual
feelings whatsoever.

———•———

It's not adultery if
I'm on a business trip.

———•———

I like BLTs too much
to give up bacon.

———•———

I follow at least six out of
the ten commandments—
that's a majority.

———•———

Even though he may hate my sins,
God will love me no matter what.

———•———

I give to the needy—
all my old clothes.

I confessed, so it's all good.

———•———

Sundays are my only
morning to sleep in!

———•———

I can't find a church in my neighborhood.

———•———

I'll go next week.

Environment

I'm just one person—I can't
make a difference.

———•———

Coordinating schedules for
carpooling is next to impossible.

———•———

The buses are full of freaks
and poor people.

———•———

I support public
transportation—for others.

I've heard those hybrids aren't
all they're cracked up to be.

———•◦•———

SUVs are safer in accidents.

———•◦•———

Every once in a while I need to
transport something big.

———•◦•———

If I ride my bicycle to work, I'll
be all sweaty when I arrive.

———•◦•———

Solar energy is too much
of an investment.

———•◦•———

I'd recycle, but it all ends up in
the same landfill anyway.

———•◦•———

Those different plastics
are so confusing.

———•◦•———

I'm too busy to notice whether the can
is marked "garbage" or "recycling."

I cash in my cans.

———•◦•———

My carbon footprint is so much
smaller than John Travolta's.

———•◦•———

I don't believe in global warming.

———•◦•———

Disposability is my
right as an American.

Tip: The Offset Excuse

Why feel bad about your eco-unfriendly
ways when all you have to do is offset your
carbon footprint? On a cross-country flight,
for example, each passenger is responsible
for the emission of 2.41 tons of CO_2. The
offset cost? A paltry \$13.28. In everyday life,
the average individual induces the emission
of 16.11 tons of CO_2 annually, but \$88.61 will
keep you guilt-free for twelve months, not to
mention allowing you to say, "I carbon-offset."

I'll start on Earth Day.

———•◦•———

We're going to destroy the earth
no matter what we do.

Life

I'm too old to go back to school.

———•◦•———

I'd never get accepted.

———•◦•———

This is just my lot in life.

———•◦•———

I'm too tired when I get home from
work to look for a better job.

———•◦•———

Nobody would ever
publish it, anyway.

———•◦•———

It's better for the kids that we
stay in a loveless marriage.

I'll never find anybody better.

<hr>

I can wait—fertility technology
is improving every day.

<hr>

The silicone might leak.

<hr>

I've lived here all my life.

<hr>

I'll do it when I've
resolved all my issues.

<hr>

I'll do it when I have more money.

<hr>

I'll do it when I lose weight.

<hr>

It's just too late.

<hr>

The key is wanting what you've got.

BEHAVING BADLY

When you face persecution or prosecution

IN THE UNITED STATES, YOU'RE
innocent until proven guilty—by
someone else. *You* may know full
well that you're guilty, but if there's
no tangible proof, you'll want to
come out swinging with excuses and
lies to suit the alleged infraction.

Especially in today's overloaded
world, we're bound to face all kinds
of accusations. Overcrowding leads

Tip: Get the Story Straight

With any excuse or lie, memory is critical. Whether your lie is challenged at a later date or you're called upon to lie in order to cover up a previous lie (a phenomenon known as the ripple effect), nothing exposes the liar like incongruous stories. If your lie involves others, make sure that you synch up—but don't match, as one of the hallmarks of group lies is verbatim recitation. For frequent fibbers, lie journals might even come in handy.

to scads of regulations designed to delimit our shrinking boundaries, while inducing frustration and hair-trigger tempers. Whether you've been busted for talking in a quiet zone, cutting in line, returning a gently used good, denying a pile of bills, or breaking the law, the most important thing to remember is that rules don't apply to you.

When delivering excuses and lies for your defense, put yourself into the mindset of the victim. Perhaps you were subject to forces beyond your control—weather, conspiracies, emergencies, or the need to get out of the grocery store really quickly despite your twenty-item basket. Individuals confronting you have no idea why you needed to do what you did—they only care about themselves.

Whatever your tactic to evade your persecutors, your goal should always be to get out of it. Sometimes this requires a good defense, while in other scenarios, turning the tables and attacking will serve you best. And when you can't come out swinging, words are all you have—the words contained in this chapter.

Cell Phones

Excuse me, but this is a
very important call.

Everyone talks and drives and
eats at the same time.

The volume control on my
phone doesn't work.

My daughter chose
that ringtone.

Everybody else seems to be enjoying
my phone-sex conversation!

My grandmother is
hard of hearing.

Sorry—it's the doctor calling
with my test results.

It's just so difficult to
turn the ringer off.

———•·•———

I've received many compliments on
my full-throated speaking voice.

———•·•———

"No cell" signs are just suggestions.

———•·•———

This movie sucks, anyway.

———•·•———

I'm just plain special.

Cutting in Line

Oh, I didn't think you were in line.

———•·•———

This is an express lane? I didn't realize.

———•·•———

My five different flavors of ice cream
and my three liters of diet soda
really count as just two items.

You're shopping for a whole battalion
and I just have this little basket.

I can't wait another
minute—I'm starving.

I left my dog in the car.

I left my children in the car.

You turned around to look at a
magazine and lost your place in line.

I just took my medication and
in a few minutes I won't be
able to drive myself home.

I asked some guy to hold my place
in line. Where did he go?

I have special needs.

I think I'm going to throw up.

I was here before you!

Returning Goods

It was broken when I got it.

It smelled like this when I got it.

Your Right to Be Wrong

In 1908, César Ritz, founder of the tony Ritz hotel chain, exclaimed, "Le client n'a jamais tort," or "The customer is never wrong." The department stores Marshall Field's and Selfridges transformed the phrase into "The customer is always right," blazing the trail for consumer power. If you don't have a ready excuse for a suspicious return, there's a fallback: you are always right, whether or not you are lying.

It didn't have tags when I bought it.

———•◦•———

What kinds of dorks
keep their receipts?

———•◦•———

I had to open it to discover
that I didn't want it!

———•◦•———

After I made a copy, I realized
I didn't need the original.

———•◦•———

I had to burn the receipt so my husband
wouldn't see how much it cost.

———•◦•———

My grandma got it
for me—'nuff said.

———•◦•———

I used it for two years
and it just didn't live up to my
wear-and-tear expectations.

———•◦•———

The technology is now obsolete.

I found it someplace
else for cheaper.

———•—•———

My dog peed on it.

Unpaid Bills

The check is in the mail.

———•—•———

I forgot to sign it? My stars, I'll
send you another one right away.

———•—•———

The bill-payer in this household
isn't here right now.

———•—•———

I bought a lottery ticket
today but I don't know yet if
I have the winning numbers.

———•—•———

I never really trusted
that Internet thingy.

Added Emphasis

When it's necessary to add credibility to your lie, it's easy to amplify your statement with one of these phrases:

"You have my word on it." • "I swear on my mother's grave." • "I swear on the life of my first-born child." • "I'm looking you in the eye." • "Now, I'm going to tell you the truth." • "If you don't believe me, you can have your money back." • "Look at this face—would I lie to you?" • "Pinky swear."

Somebody in your office gave me the wrong address.

I've been out of town on a human-rights mission.

Clearly, it's identity theft!

I forgot to carry the zero.

Someone must have accidentally
thrown that bill away.

———•—•———

Workplace harassment exacerbated
stress-related medical problems,
necessitating my going out on
disability leave, compounded by
misdiagnosed and untreated learning
disabilities, causing me to have no
income. In short, I can't pay you.

———•—•———

That bill was really confusing.

———•—•———

I ended that service months ago.

———•—•———

"Neither snow nor rain nor heat nor
gloom of night stays these couriers
from the swift completion of their
appointed rounds"? That's a damned lie.

———•—•———

The symbol "$" is undefined
and ambiguous.

Automotive Mishaps

If we weren't supposed to text
while driving, God wouldn't have
made cell phones so portable.

———•—•———

The tree came out of nowhere.

———•—•———

The sun was in my eyes.

———•—•———

The gas and the brake are
so hard to tell apart!

———•—•———

I think I just had my first
out-of-body experience.

———•—•———

That pedestrian totally
dive-bombed my vehicle.

———•—•———

It all happened in an instant
when I sneezed.

There was a bee in the car.

———•❖•———

A really awful song came on the
radio and I had to change it—fast.

———•❖•———

I was just going with the flow of traffic.

———•❖•———

That yellow did *not* last the
legally required duration.

———•❖•———

I was being chased!

———•❖•———

I'm a big supporter of the
Police Athletic League.

Getting Busted

Isn't Long Island
Iced Tea nonalcoholic?

———•❖•———

My juice must have accidentally
fermented in the cupholder.

I didn't realize the Oxycodone
would affect me that way.

———•••———

My girlfriend, Foxy, was just looking
for change down there. We didn't
want to get a parking ticket.

———•••———

I just get turned on by sex in public.

———•••———

I'm on chemo and you wouldn't
believe how nauseated I get.

———•••———

Just because it's in my hand
doesn't mean I inhaled.

———•••———

It *should* be legal.

———•••———

I can't imagine *who* would have hid a
kilo of cocaine in my carry-on bag.

———•••———

His face got in the way of
my fist, repeatedly.

It was clearly self-defense.

When I pointed it at the shopkeeper
I had no idea it was loaded.

Not only was I feeling especially insane
temporarily, I'm pretty crazy in general.

It was an honest mistake.

Tip: Take Action

When you're caught in questionable circum-
stances, words alone may not be enough to
deter negative consequences. To ensure your
safety, you'll want an arsenal of behaviors to
support your story. With a sickness claim, gag
or sneeze. Validate a worst-day-of-your-life
excuse with deep, crushing sobs. Underscore
"I'm scared" with uncontrollable shaking. As a
last-ditch effort, peeing in your pants will get
you out of almost anything.

FAMOUSLY
INFAMOUS

When the stakes are high

EVERYBODY WANTS TO BE FAMOUS
these days, whether via reality television or for actual accomplishments.
If they can't be famous, they want to
look, dress, and act the part—and
what better way than through
excuses and lies? It's comforting
to know that it's not just the little
guy making stuff up. Everyone
does it, including—or perhaps
especially—those at the top.

Liar, Liar, Pants on Fire

Pathological lying, AKA pseudologia phantastica, has long been viewed as a symptom of an underlying mental disorder. A coping mechanism from early childhood, pathological lying tends to be unplanned, impulsive, and goal oriented. Pathological liars often believe their own lies (and thus can pass polygraphs). It may be partly physiological: one study suggests that these liars' brains have 26 percent more white matter, which has been linked with lying ability.

Where the previous chapters have provided actual verbiage for your daily usage, here you will find inspiration for the moments when you need to go off script. The corporate section yields insight into how these companies got so big in the first place—lies and excuses helped. Sports present front-row opportunities to use performance-enhancing drugs and to gamble—and then lie about it. Among entertainers, there's little more entertaining than watching someone spiral out of control—and then attempt to spin it. For those in the fourth estate, keeping the beast fed with media coverage necessitates plagiarism. Presidents and other politicians provide a great example, mastering the art of spin, cover-ups, and the ultimate excuse: "national security." The criminals are a sad bunch; unfortunately, even though they excused and lied their hearts out, they got caught, and some even got punished.

The lesson to gather from all these big shots is never to give yourself away. If you do something wrong, lie—whether or not you are under oath. If all else fails, you can always plead insanity.

Corporate

"There is no proof that cigarette smoking is one of the causes [of lung cancer]. We believe the products we make are not injurious to health." —Tobacco Industry Research Committee, January 4, 1954

———•◦•———

"It depends on your definition of asleep. They were not stretched out. They had their eyes closed. They were seated at their desks with their heads in a nodding position." —John Hogan, Commonwealth Edison supervisor, in defense of nuclear power plant operators charged with sleeping on the job, 1980

———•◦•———

"Chromium in this form is a naturally occurring metal that is an essential ingredient in the human diet, one that is often included in multiple vitamin/mineral supplements." —Pacific Gas and Electric flyer, reassuring residents of Hinkley, California, who were living in deadly polluted areas, 1988

"He was obsessed to the point that it interfered with his judgment. The money was used to purchase and resell antique clocks ... This isn't an excuse or defense for what he did." —Attorney Justin P. Walder, in defense of Francis X. Vitale Jr., who embezzled $12.5 million from Engelhard Corporation, 1997

"The third quarter is looking great." —Kenneth Lay, Enron chairman, just months before the company reported a $638 million third-quarter loss, September 2001

"I have done nothing wrong." —Martha Stewart, after being convicted of lying to investigators, 2004

"He was cruising on adult Web sites." —Attorney Max Blecher, explaining that Peter Murnane, CFO of Mesa Air, was simply trying to delete porn when documents relevant to a lawsuit were deleted, 2007

Sports

"Being a knuckleball pitcher, I sometimes have to file my nails between innings, so I carry an emery board to the mound." —Joe Niekro, Minnesota Twins pitcher, explaining why he had an emery board and sandpaper in his pocket while pitching against the Anaheim Angels, 1987

"Although I truly believe this encounter between us was consensual, I recognize now that she did not and does not view this incident the same way I did." —Kobe Bryant, basketball player, apologizing to the woman who accused him of rape, 2004

"I have never, ever used performance-enhancing drugs." —Marion Jones, Olympic gold-medal runner, four years before being sentenced to prison for lying to federal investigators about her drug use, 2004

"My lawyers have advised me that I cannot answer these questions without jeopardizing my friends, my family, and myself." —Mark McGwire, baseball player, to Congress, concerning his steroid use, March 17, 2005

"I bet on my team to win every night because I love my team." —Pete Rose, baseball player and manager, admitting to betting in the 1980s, 2007

Truthiness

Truthiness, Merriam-Webster's 2006 Word of the Year, is defined as "truth that comes from the gut, not books." The term was popularized when its creator, comedian and television host Stephen Colbert, satirized politicians who eschew intellectual reasoning when making important decisions. Use truthiness in your own repertoire of lying techniques: simply go by the truth that feels right rather than bothering with facts or empirical evidence.

"I am committed to examining my feelings and will recognize, appreciate, and respect the differences among people in our society." —Tim Hardaway, basketball player, apologizing for exposing his homophobia, 2007

Entertainment

"The heart wants what it wants."
—Woody Allen, on why he felt it was fine to marry his stepdaughter Soon-Yi, 1992

"I think you know in life what's a good thing to do and what's a bad thing, and I did a bad thing."
—Hugh Grant on *The Tonight Show*, discussing his arrest on lewd conduct charges, 1995

"I would never intentionally endanger the lives of my children."
—Michael Jackson, apologizing for dangling his baby outside a Berlin hotel window, 2002

"I was told that I should shoplift. The director said I should try it out." —Colleen Rainey, Saks Fifth Avenue guard, quoting Winona Ryder's explanation for shoplifting, 2002

———◆———

"Personally, I'd never lip-synch. It's just not me." —Ashlee Simpson, before her lip-synching was revealed on a botched *Saturday Night Live* appearance, 2004

———◆———

"I am sorry if anyone was offended by the wardrobe malfunction during the halftime performance at the Super Bowl. It was not intentional and is regrettable." —Justin Timberlake, after exposing Janet Jackson's breast to an estimated 140 million viewers, 2004

———◆———

"Hatred of any kind goes against my faith." —Mel Gibson, regarding his anti-Semitic remarks to a law-enforcement officer, 2006

The Well-Planned Hoax

Successful hoaxes require skillful planning and execution, whether a brilliant forgery, a book-length lie, a fake anthropological find, or a false headline (such as the 1957 British news report on that year's bumper spaghetti harvest—from trees). The best of the best? Orson Welles's 1938 *The War of the Worlds*, a phony news broadcast about aliens landing on Earth that prompted unprecedented terror in the radio-listening audience.

"[I was] starving because I had not ate all day and possibly speeding a little bit . . . and I wanted to have an In-N-Out burger . . . [I'd had] one margarita at the event." —Paris Hilton, on why she got popped for drunk driving, 2006

"I probably did take my new-found freedom a little too far." —Britney Spears, after several indiscretions were captured by the media, 2006

Media

"I have become so numb to the horrific things that happen in this world that I sometimes forget that there are still people who feel." —Marconi, Portland, Oregon radio host, apologizing for broadcasting a tape of an Iraqi beheading and joking about it, 2004

"Mental illness is—you know, it does not necessarily mean that you're incapable of doing creative or interesting things." —Jayson Blair, *New York Times* reporter, excusing his plagiarism of dozens of articles, 2004

"I was a bad guy. If I was gonna write a book that was true, and I was gonna write a book that was honest, then I was gonna have to write about myself in very, very negative ways." —James Frey to Oprah Winfrey, before much of his book chronicling his life as an addict and in jail was exposed as fiction, 2005

"[I] can honestly say that any phrasing similarities between her works and mine were completely unintentional and unconscious." —Kaavya Viswanathan, Harvard student, regarding the plagiarism of one of several sources for her debut novel, 2006

———•◦•———

"Let me provide a context . . . not as an excuse . . . [B]ut there is a difference between premeditated murder and a gun going off accidentally." —Don Imus, justifying his racist comments about the Rutgers women's basketball team, 2007

U.S. Presidents

"No American boy is going to fight a war on foreign soil." —Franklin D. Roosevelt, two years before sending Americans to fight in Europe, 1940

"The world will note that the first atomic bomb was dropped on Hiroshima, a military base. That was because we wished in this first attack to avoid, insofar as possible, the killing of civilians." —Harry S. Truman, radio address, August 9, 1945

"People have got to know whether or not their President is a crook. Well, I'm not a crook." —Richard Nixon, denying any involvement in the Watergate scandal, 1973

"[W]e did not—repeat, did not—trade weapons or anything else for hostages, nor will we." —Ronald Reagan, four months before admitting otherwise, November 1986

"Read my lips: no new taxes." —George H. W. Bush to the Republican Convention, three years before raising income taxes and levies, 1988

"I did not have sexual relations with that woman, Miss Lewinsky." —Bill Clinton, denying allegations of infidelity in the White House, 1998

"We found the weapons of mass destruction. We found biological laboratories." —George W. Bush, before Secretary of State Colin Powell acknowledged that WMD were not found in Iraq, 2003

Other Politicos

"I haven't committed a crime. What I did was fail to comply with the law." —David Dinkins, New York City mayor, downplaying five years of tax evasion, 1973

"I didn't accept it. I received it." —Richard Allen, national security advisor, explaining a $1,000 gift for arranging for a private interview with Nancy Reagan, 1981

"He didn't say that. He read what was given to him in a speech." —Richard G. Darman, budget director, explaining why President George H. W. Bush was breaking a campaign pledge about wetland preservation, 1992

"There was a real lack of situational awareness."—Michael Chertoff, secretary of homeland security, regarding the slow response to Hurricane Katrina, 2005

Supersize It

The many compelling reasons to become famous include the chance to tell a "big lie," an intentional distortion of the truth for public propaganda. Most prevaricators only work one-on-one, but with the big lie, millions can be deceived. No lesser liar than Adolf Hitler stated, "In the big lie there is always a certain force of credibility . . . [people] would not believe that others could have the impudence to distort the truth so infamously."

"My days are incredible, you know: work, politics, troubles, moving around, public exams that never end, a life under constant pressure." —Silvio Berlusconi, former premier of Italy, justifying his flirtatious ways to his wife, 2007

"I have a wide stance when going to the bathroom." —Larry Craig, congressman, denying claims of soliciting sex in a Minneapolis airport bathroom, 2007

Criminals

"Whether or not ingestion of [sugar] foodstuff . . . causes you to alter your personality somehow, or causes you to act in an aggressive manner, I don't know . . . But there is a minority opinion in psychiatric fields that there is some connection." —Attorney Douglas Schmidt, in the infamous "Twinkie defense" of Dan White, who shot and killed San Francisco Mayor George Moscone and Supervisor Harvey Milk, 1979

"He always have orgasm and he doesn't wait for me to have orgasm. He's selfish. I don't think it's fair." —Lorena Bobbitt, commenting to police after her arrest for severing her husband's penis, 1993

"We killed our parents because we were afraid." —Erik Menendez, claiming the "abuse excuse," 1995

"It was wrong and I am sorry. I give you my word that it will not happen again." —Mary Kay Letourneau, less than a month before she was caught with fourteen-year-old Vili, again, 1997

"God, I hope she is found alive." —Scott Peterson, months before being convicted of the murder of his pregnant wife, 2003

"I did not have anything to do with these murders. Ever." —O. J. Simpson, ten years after the murders of Nicole Brown and Ron Goldman, 2004

"These are the best years of your life."